Introduction

Thank you for choosing this book, containing 365 inspirational quotes.

The quotes within the following pages come from a wide variety of influential and inspiring people. There are quotes from ancient philosophers such as Socrates, as well as quotes from modern day celebrities such as Oprah Winfrey!

You might like to read one quote each day for a whole year, or perhaps, simply open this book to a random page whenever you require a boost of motivation.

Whichever way you choose to use this book, I hope you enjoy the quotes contained within and that they can help spur you on to do great things!

Once again, thanks for picking up this book, I hope you enjoy it!

365 Inspirational Quotes

1.

"Act as if what you do makes a difference. IT DOES."

- William James

2.

"Success is not final, failure is not fatal: it is the courage to continue that counts."

- Winston Churchill

3.

"Never bend your head. Always hold it high. Look the world straight in the eye."

- Helen Keller

4.

"What you get by achieving your goals is not as important as what you become by achieving your goals."

- Zig Ziglar

5.

"Believe you can, and you're halfway there."

- Theodore Roosevelt

6.

"Don't give up, don't take anything personally, and don't take no for an answer."

- Sophia Amoruso

7.

"Work hard in silence. Let your success be your noise."

- Frank Ocean

8.

"You can, you should, and if you're brave enough to start, you will."

- Stephen King

9.

"Attitude is the difference between an ordeal and an adventure."

- Bob Bitchin

10.

"Failure is a bruise, not a tattoo."

- Jon Sinclair

11.

"All our dreams can come true, if we have the courage to pursue them."

- Walt Disney

12.

"The secret of getting ahead is getting started."

- Mark Twain

13.

"The best time to plant a tree was 20 years ago. The second-best time is now."

- Chinese Proverb

14.

"Don't limit yourself. Many people limit themselves to what they think they can do. You can go as far as your mind lets you. What you believe, remember, you can achieve."

- Mary Kay Ash

15.

"It's hard to beat a person who never gives up."

- Babe Ruth

16.

"When you have a dream, you've got to grab it and never let go."

- Carol Burnett

17.

"I can't change the direction of the wind, but I can adjust my sails to always reach my destination."

- Jimmy Dean

18.

"No matter what you're going through, there's a light at the end of the tunnel."

- Demi Lovato

19.

"It is our attitude at the beginning of a difficult task which, more than anything else, will affect its successful outcome."

- William James

20.

"Life is like riding a bicycle. To keep your balance, you must keep moving."

- Albert Einstein

21.

"It's not what we have in life, but who we have in our life that matters."

- Unknown

22.

"Work like there is someone working twenty-four hours a day to take it away from you."

- Mark Cuban

23.

"Do what you have to do until you can do what you want to do."

- Oprah Winfrey

24.

"Find something you're passionate about and keep tremendously interested in it."

- Julia Child

25.

"It always seems impossible until it's done."

- Nelson Mandela

26.

"If people are doubting how far you can go, go so far that you can't hear them anymore."

- Michele Ruiz

27.

"We need to accept that we won't always make the right decisions, that we'll screw up royally sometimes – understanding that failure is not the opposite of success, it's part of success."

- Arianna Huffington

28.

"Write it. Shoot it. Publish it. Crochet it, sauté it, whatever. MAKE."

- Josh Whedon

29.

"You've gotta dance like there's nobody watching, love like you'll never be hurt, sing like there's nobody listening, and live like it's heaven on earth."

- William P. Purkey

30.

"Fairy tales are more than true: not because they tell us that dragons exists, but because they tell us that dragons can be beaten."

- Neil Gaiman

31.

"Just don't give up trying to do what you really want to do. When there is love and inspiration, I don't think you can go wrong."

- Ella Fitzgerald

32.

"Limit your 'always' and your 'nevers'."

- Amy Poehler

33.

"Nothing is impossible. The word itself says 'I'M POSSIBLE'."

- Audrey Hepburn

34.

"You are never too old to set another goal or to dream a new dream."

- C.S. Lewis

35.

"Try to be a rainbow in someone else's cloud."

- Maya Angelou

36.

"If opportunity doesn't knock, build a door."

- Unknown

37.

"What seems to us as bitter trials are often blessings in disguise."

- Oscar Wilde

38.

"You don't need a new day to start over, you only need a new mindset."

- Hazel Hira Ozbek

39.

"It's kind of fun to do the impossible."

- Walt Disney

40.

"Doubt kills more dreams than failure ever will."

- Suzy Kassem

41.

"Everything you can imagine is real."

- Pablo Picasso

42.

"When one door of happiness closes, another opens; but often we look so long at the closed door that we do not see the one which has been opened for us."

- Helen Keller

43.

"Do one thing every day that scares you."

- Eleanor Roosevelt

44.

"Smart people learn from everything and everyone, average people from their experiences, stupid people already have all the answers."

- Socrates

45.

"Do what you feel in your heart to be right – for you'll be criticized anyway."

- Eleanor Roosevelt

46.

"You do not find the happy life. You make it."

- Camilla Eyring Kimball

47.

"Inspiration comes from within yourself. One has to be positive. When you're positive, good things happen."

- Deep Roy

48.

"Sometimes you will never know the value of a moment until it becomes a memory."

- Dr. Seuss

49.

"You must do the things you think you cannot do."

- Eleanor Roosevelt

50.

"It isn't where you came from. It's where you're going that counts."

- Ella Fitzgerald

51.

"We have to choose joy and keep choosing it."

- Henri J.M. Nouwen

52.

"Always be a work in progress."

- Emily Lillian

53.

"The man who moves a mountain begins by carrying away small stones."

- Confucius

54.

"There are secret opportunities inside every failure."

- Unknown

55.

"Start today, not tomorrow. If anything, you should have started yesterday."

- Emil Motycka

56.

"Happiness is not something ready-made. It comes from your own actions."

- Dalai Lama XIV

57.

"Whatever you are, be a good one."

- Abraham Lincoln

58.

"The same boiling water that softens the potato hardens the egg. It's what you're made of, not the circumstances."

- Unknown

59.

"If we have the attitude that it's going to be a great day, it usually is."

- Catherine Pulsifier

60.

"You can either experience the pain of discipline or the pain of regret. The choice is yours."

- Unknown

61.

"It is never too late to be what you might have been."

- George Eliot

62.

"Stay close to anything that makes you glad you are alive."

- Hafez

63.

"You get what you give."

- Jennifer Lopez

64.

"Happiness often sneaks in through a door you didn't know you left open."

- John Barrymore

65.

"We must be willing to let go of the life we planned so as to have the life that is waiting for us."

- Joseph Campbell

66.

"We are what we repeatedly do."

- Aristotle

67.

"The future belongs to those who believe in the beauty of their dreams."

- Eleanor Roosevelt

68.

"If you are always trying to be normal, you will never know how amazing you can be."

- Maya Angelou

69.

"Whatever you do today is important because you are exchanging a day of your life for it."

- Unknown

70.

"A goal is not always meant to be reached. It often serves simply as something to aim at."

- Bruce Lee

71.

"Impossible is just an opinion."

- Paulo Coelho

72.

"Your passion is waiting for your courage to catch up."

- Isabelle Lafleche

73.

"Magic is believing in yourself. If you can make that happen, you can make anything happen."

- Johann Wolfgang Von Goethe

74.

"If something is important enough, even if the odds are stacked against you, you should still do it."

- Elon Musk

75.

"Hold the vision, trust the process."

- Unknown

76.

"Happiness is not by chance, but by choice."

- Jim Rohn

77.

"Life changes very quickly, in a very positive way, if you let it."

- Lindsey Vonn

78.

"Keep your face to the sunshine, and you cannot see a shadow."

- Helen Keller

79.

"Never limit yourself because of others' limited imagination; never limit others because of your own limited imagination."

- Mae Jemison

80.

"Be the change that you wish to see in the world."

- Mahatma Gandhi

81.

"Whatever the problem, be part of the solution. Don't just sit around raising questions and pointing out obstacles."

- Tina Fey

82.

"If you haven't found it yet, keep looking."

- Steve Jobs

83.

"You can't do anything about the length of your life, but you can do something about its width and depth."

- Evan Esar

84.

"The struggle you're in today is developing the strength you need for tomorrow."

- Unknown

85.

"If you get tired, learn to rest, not to quit."

- Banksy

86.

"Don't be afraid to give up the good to go for the great."

- John D. Rockefeller

87.

"People who wonder if the glass is half-full or half-empty miss the point. The glass is refillable."

- Unknown

88.

"No one is to blame for your future situation but yourself. If you want to be successful, then become successful."

- Jaymin Shah

89.

"Things come to those who wait, but only the things left by those who hustle."

- Abraham Lincoln

90.

"Invest in your dreams. Grind now, shine later."

- Unknown

91.

"Let us make our future now, and let us make our dreams tomorrow's reality."

- Malala Yousafzai

92.

"You don't always need a plan. Sometimes you just need to breathe, trust, let go, and see what happens."

- Mandy Hale

93.

"If I cannot do great things, I can do small things in a great way."

- Martin Luther King Jr.

94.

"My mission in life is not merely to survive, but to THRIVE."

- Maya Angelou

95.

"The bad news is time flies. The good news is you're the pilot."

- Michael Altshuler

96.

"The true sign of intelligence isn't knowledge, but imagination."

- Albert Einstein

97.

"Time has a wonderful way of showing us what really matters."

- Margaret Peters

98.

"We are only as blind as we want to be."

- Maya Angelou

99.

"Courage is knowing what not to fear."

- Plato

100.

"Life goes by fast. Enjoy it. Calm down. It's all funny."

- Joan Rivers

101.

"Every successful person in the world is a hustler in one way or another. We all hustle to get where we need to be. Only a fool would sit around and wait on another man to feed him."

- K'wan

102.

"Hustlers don't sleep, they nap."

- Unknown

103.

"Without hustle, talent will only carry you so far."

- Gary Vaynerchuk

104.

"How wonderful is it that nobody need wait a single moment before starting to improve the world."

- Anne Frank

105.

"Some people want it to happen, some wish it would happen, others make it happen."

- Michael Jordan

106.

"Don't wait. The time will never be just right."

- Napoleon Hill

107.

"Life has got all those twists and turns. You've got to hold on tight and off you go."

- Nicole Kidman

108.

"Inspiration is some mysterious blessing which happens when the wheels are turning smoothly."

- Quentin Blake

109.

"With the right kind of coaching and determination, you can accomplish anything."

- Reese Witherspoon

110.

"If you have good thoughts, they will shine out of your face like sunbeams, and you will always look lovely."

- Roald Dahl

111.

"You don't have a soul. You are a soul. You have a body."

- C.S. Lewis

112.

"Kindness is a language the blind can see and the deaf can hear."

- Mark Twain

113.

"Never let your fear decide your future."

- Unknown

114.

"Life is very short. Insecurity is a waste of time."

- Diane Von Furstenberg

115.

"Don't wait for opportunity. Create it."

- Unknown

116.

"Great things are done by a series of small things brought together."

- Vincent Van Gogh

117.

"Very often, a change of self is needed more than a change of scene."

- A.C. Benson

118.

"It's not the load that breaks you, it's the way you carry out."

- Lou Holtz

119.

"The hard days are what make you stronger."

- Aly Raisman

120.

"If you believe it'll work out, you'll see opportunities. If you don't believe it'll work out, you'll see obstacles."

- Wayne Dyer

121.

"No matter what people tell you, words and ideas can change the world."

- Robin Williams

122.

"Each person must live their life as a model for others."

- Rosa Parks

123.

"A champion is defined not by their wins, but by how they can recover when they fall."

- Serena Williams

124.

"Motivation comes from working on things we care about."
- Sheryl Sandberg

125.

"There are only two options: make progress or make excuses."
- Unknown

126.

"Do not judge me by my successes, judge me by how many times I fell down and got back up again."
- Nelson Mandela

127.

"The best way to predict the future is to create it."

- Peter Drucker

128.

"You are what you do, not what you say you'll do."

- Unknown

129.

"No amount of security is worth the suffering of a mediocre life chained to a routine that has killed your dreams."

- Maya Mendoza

130.

"Be so good they can't ignore you."

- Steve Martin

131.

"Keep your eyes on the stars, and your feet on the ground."

- Theodore Roosevelt

132.

"You can waste your life drawing lines. Or you can live your life crossing them."

- Shonda Rhimes

133.

"You've got to get up every morning with determination if you're going to go to bed with satisfaction."

- George Lorimer

134.

"In a gentle way, you can shake the world."

- Mahatma Gandhi

135.

"Don't be pushed around by the fears in your mind. Be led by the dreams in your heart."

- Roy T. Bennett

136.

"Most people fail not because they lack the skills or aptitude to reach their goal, but because they simply don't believe they can reach it."

- Tim Ferriss

137.

"Winners never quit, and quitters never win."

- Vince Lombardi

138.

"I have not failed. I've just found 10,000 ways that won't work."

- Thomas Edison

139.

"Courage is being scared to death... and saddling up anyway."

- John Wayne

140.

"Wealth is not about having a lot of money, it's about having a lot of options."

- Chris Rock

141.

"Don't say you don't have enough time. You have exactly the same number of hours per day that were given to Helen Keller, Pasteur, Michelangelo, Mother Teresa, Leonardo Da Vinci, Thomas Jefferson, and Albert Einstein."

- H. Jackson Brown Jr.

142.

"Hard work beats talent when talent doesn't work hard."

- Tim Notke

143.

"If everything seems to be under control, you're not going fast enough."

- Mario Andretti

144.

"Opportunity is missed by most people because it is dressed in overalls and looks like work."

- Thomas Edison

145.

"The only difference between ordinary and extraordinary is that little extra."

- Jimmy Johnson

146.

"The best way to appreciate your job is to imagine yourself without one."

- Oscar Wilde

147.

"Unsuccessful people make their decisions based on their current situations. Successful people make their decisions based on where they want to be."

- Benjamin Hardy

148.

"Ambition is the first step to success. The second step is action."

- Unknown

149.

"People are rewarded in public for what they've practiced for years in private."

- Tony Robbins

150.

"If you don't sacrifice for what you want, what you want becomes the sacrifice."

- Unknown

151.

"Never stop doing your best just because someone doesn't give you credit."

- Kamari aka Lyrikal

152.

"Work hard for what you want because it won't come to you without a fight. You have to be strong and courageous and know that you can do anything you put your mind to. If somebody puts you down or criticizes you, just keep on believing in yourself and turn it into something positive."

- Leah LaBelle

153.

"Work hard, be kind, and amazing things will happen."

- Conan O'Brien

154.

"Never give up on a dream just because of the time it will take to accomplish it. The time will pass anyway."

- Earl Nightingale

155.

"If you work on something a little bit every day, you end up with something that is massive."

- Kenneth Goldsmith

156.

"If you are on the right path, it will always be uphill."

- Henry B. Eyring

157.

"You have been criticizing yourself for years, and it hasn't worked. Try approving of yourself and see what happens."

- Louise L. Hay

158.

"Anything's possible if you've got enough nerve."

- J.K. Rowling

159.

"I never dreamed about success. I worked for it."

- Estee Lauder

160.

"What is done in love is done well."

- Vincent Van Gogh

161.

"The big secret in life is that there is no secret. Whatever your goal, you can get there if you're willing to work."

- Oprah Winfrey

162.

"Never allow a person to tell you no who doesn't have the power to say yes."

- Eleanor Roosevelt

163.

"At any given moment, you have the power to say: this is not how the story is going to end."

- Unknown

164.

"Amateurs sit around and wait for inspiration. The rest of us get up and go to work."

- Stephen King

165.

"Your work is going to fill a large part of your life, and the only way to be truly satisfied is to do what you believe is great work. And the only way to do great work is to love what you do. If you haven't found it yet, keep looking."

- Steve Jobs

166.

"Rule your mind or it will rule you."

- Buddha

167.

"If it doesn't challenge you, it doesn't change you."

- Unknown

168.

"Learn the rules like a pro, so you can break them like an artist."

- Pablo Picasso

169.

"It isn't what we say or think that defines us, but what we do."

- Jane Austen

170.

"Do what you love, and success will follow. Passion is the fuel behind a successful career."

- Meg Whitman

171.

"Nothing will work unless you do."

- Maya Angelou

172.

"Sometimes when you're in a dark place you think you've been buried, but you've actually been planted."

- Christine Caine

173.

"Don't limit your challenges. Challenge your limits."

- Unknown

174.

"Whenever you find yourself doubting how far you can go, just remember how far you have come."

- Unknown

175.

"Everyone has inside them a piece of good news. The good news is you don't know how good you can be! How much you can love! What you can accomplish! And what your potential is!"

- Anne Frank

176.

"It is impossible to live without failing at something, unless you live so cautiously that you might as well not have lived at all, in which case you have failed by default."

- J.K. Rowling

177.

"You don't learn to walk by following rules. You learn by doing and falling over.

- Richard Branson

178.

"Success is never owned. It's rented, and the rent is due every day."

- Unknown

179.

"Do what you can, with what you have, where you are."

- Theodore Roosevelt

180.

"Happiness is when what you think, what you say, and what you do are in harmony."

- Mahatma Gandhi

181.

"Some luck lies in not getting what you thought you wanted but getting what you have, which once you have got it you may be smart enough to see it is what you would have wanted had you known."

- Garrison Keillor

182.

"Don't quit yet, the worst moments are usually followed by the most beautiful silver linings. You have to stay strong, remember to keep your head up and remain hopeful."

- Unknown

183.

"When written in Chinese, the word 'crisis' is composed of two characters – one represents danger and the other represents opportunity."

- John F. Kennedy

184.

"Good. Better. Best. Never let it rest. 'Til your good is better and your better is best."

- St. Jerome

185.

"In the middle of every difficulty lies opportunity."

- Albert Einstein

186.

"Be in love with your life. Every minute of it."

- Jack Kerouac

187.

"When you have a bad day, a really bad day, try and treat the world better than it treated you."

- Patrick Stump

188.

"You are allowed to be both a masterpiece and a work in progress, simultaneously."

- Sophia Bush

189.

"Go the extra mile, it's never crowded there."

- Dr. Wayne D. Dyer

190.

"Fortune favors the bold who get shit done."

- Sophia Amoruso

191.

"Dreams don't work unless you do."

- John C. Maxwell

192.

"Make each day your masterpiece."

- John Wooden

193.

"Wherever you go, go with all your heart."

- Confucius

194.

"Turn your wounds in to wisdom."

- Oprah Winfrey

195.

"We can do anything we want to if we stick to it long enough."

- Helen Keller

196.

"Success is 99.9% an inside job."

- Emily Williams

197.

"If you are always trying to be normal, you will never know how amazing you can be."

- Maya Angelou

198.

"Don't decrease the goal. Increase the effort."

- Unknown

199.

"Success isn't overnight. It's when every day you get a little better than before. It adds up."

- Dwayne Johnson

200.

"Your life isn't yours if you always care what others think."

- Unknown

201.

"Success is no accident. It is hard work, perseverance, learning, studying, sacrifice, and most of all, love what you are learning to do."

- Pele

202.

"Would you like me to give you a formula for success? It's quite simple, really: Double your rate of failure. You are thinking of failure as the enemy of success. But it isn't at all. You can be discouraged by failure or you can learn from it, so go ahead and make mistakes. Make all you can. Because remember, that's where you will find success."

- Thomas J. Watson

203.

"Every champion was once a contender that didn't give up."

- Gabby Douglas

204.

"To be a champion, I think you have to see the big picture. It's not about winning and losing; it's about every day hard work and about thriving on a challenge. It's about embracing the pain that you'll experience at the end of a race and not being afraid. I think people think too hard and get afraid of a certain challenge."

- Summer Sanders

205.

"Don't dream about success. Get out there and work for it."

- Unknown

206.

"The pessimist sees difficulty in every opportunity. The optimist sees opportunity in every difficulty."

- Winston Churchill

207.

"Don't let yesterday take up too much of today."

- Will Rogers

208.

"You learn more from failure than from success. Don't let it stop you. Failure builds character."

- Unknown

209.

"It's not whether you get knocked down, it's whether you get up."

- Vince Lombardi

210.

"If you are working on something that you really care about, you don't have to be pushed. The vision pulls you."

- Steve Jobs

211.

"I hated every minute of training, but I said: don't quit. Suffer now and live the rest of your life as a champion."

- Muhammad Ali

212.

"Opportunities don't happen. You create them."

- Chris Grosser

213.

"Success is liking yourself, liking what you do, and liking how you do it."

- Maya Angelou

214.

"If you obey all the rules, you miss all the fun."

- Katharine Hepburn

215.

"Life is not what you alone make it. Life is the input of everyone who touched your life and every experience that entered it. We are all part of one another."

- Yuri Kochiyama

216.

"People who are crazy enough to think they can change the world, are the ones who do."

- Rob Siltanen

217.

"Failure will never overtake me if my determination to succeed is strong enough."

- Og Mandino

218.

"We may encounter many defeats, but we must not be defeated."

- Maya Angelou

219.

"Knowing is not enough; we must apply. Wishing is not enough; we must do."

- Johann Wolfgang Von Goethe

220.

"Imagine your life is perfect in every respect; what would it look like?"

- Brian Tracy

221.

"When you reach the end of your rope, tie a knot and hang out."

- Abraham Lincoln

222.

"Never regret anything that made you smile."

- Mark Twain

223.

"You must do the thing you think you cannot do."

- Eleanor Roosevelt

224.

"If you want to fly, give up everything that weighs you down."

- Buddha

225.

"I never lose. Either I win or I learn."

- Nelson Mandela

226.

"We generate fears while we sit. We overcome them by action."

- Dr. Henry Link

227.

"Whether you think you can or think you can't, you're right."

- Henry Ford

228.

"Security is mostly a superstition. Life is either a daring adventure or nothing."

- Helen Keller

229.

"The man who has confidence in himself gains the confidence of others."

- Hasidic Proverb

230.

"The only limit to our realization of tomorrow will be our doubts of today."

- Franklin D. Roosevelt

231.

"Today is your opportunity to build the tomorrow you want."

- Ken Poirot

232.

"Getting over a painful experience is much like crossing the monkey bars. You have to let go at some point in order to move forward."

- C.S. Lewis

233.

"Focus on being productive instead of busy."

- Tim Ferriss

234.

"You don't need to see the whole staircase, just take the first step."

- Martin Luther King Jr.

235.

"It's not all sunshine and rainbows, but a good amount of it actually is."

- Unknown

236.

"Creativity is intelligence having fun."

- Albert Einstein

237.

"What you lack in talent can be made up with desire, hustle, and giving 110% all the time."

- Don Zimmer

238.

"Develop an attitude of gratitude. Say thank you to everyone you meet for everything they do for you."

- Brian Tracy

239.

"To see what is right and not do it is a lack of courage."

- Confucius

240.

"Fake it until you make it! Act as if you had all the confidence you require until it becomes your reality."

- Brian Tracy

241.

"If you're too comfortable, it's time to move on. Terrified of what's next? You're on the right track."

- Susan Fales-Hill

242.

"Sunshine all the time makes a desert."

- Arabic Proverb

243.

"The big lesson in life is never be scared of anyone or anything."

- Frank Sinatra

244.

"You're so much stronger than your excuses."

- Unknown

245.

"I choose to make the rest of my life, the best of my life."

- Louise Hay

246.

"The future belongs to the competent. Get good, get better, be the best!"

- Brian Tracy

247.

"For every reason it's not possible, there are hundreds of people who have faced the same circumstances and succeeded."

- Jack Canfield

248.

"Things work out best for those who make the best of how things work out."

- John Wooden

249.

"I think goals should never be easy, they should force you to work, even if they are uncomfortable at the time."

- Michael Phelps

250.

"One of the lessons that I grew up with was to always stay true to yourself and never let what somebody else says distract you from your goals."

- Michelle Obama

251.

"Nothing can dim the light that shines from within."

- Maya Angelou

252.

"Be so good they can't ignore you."

- Steve Martin

253.

"This is a reminder for you to create your own rule book, and live your life the way you want it."

- Reese Evans

254.

"If you don't get out of the box you've been raised in, you won't understand how much bigger the world is."

- Angelina Jolie

255.

"Do the best you can. No one can do more than that."

- John Wooden

256.

"Today's accomplishments were yesterday's impossibilities."

- Robert H. Schuller

257.

"You don't have to be great to start, but you have to start to be great."

- Zig Ziglar

258.

"A clear vision, backed by definite plans, gives you a tremendous feeling of confidence and personal power."

- Brian Tracy

259.

"There are no limits to what you can accomplish, except the limits you place on your own thinking."

- Brian Tracy

260.

"Start by doing what's necessary; then do what's possible; and suddenly you are doing the impossible."

- Francis of Assisi

261.

"It's never too late to be what you might've been."
- George Eliot

262.

"If you can dream it, you can do it."
- Walt Disney

263.

"Trust yourself that you can do it and get it."
- Baz Luhrmann

264.

"Don't let what you can't do interfere with what you can do."

- Unknown

265.

"You can do anything you set your mind to."

- Benjamin Franklin

266.

"We know what we are, but not what we may be."

- William Shakespeare

267.

"Perfection is not attainable, but if we chase perfection, we can catch excellence."

- Vince Lombardi

268.

"Do your little bit of good where you are; it's those little bits of good put together that overwhelm the world."

- Desmond Tutu

269.

"It is during our darkest moments that we must focus to see the light."

- Aristotle

270.

"We must let go of the life we have planned, so as to accept the one that is waiting for us."

- Joseph Campbell

271.

"All we can do is the best we can do."

- David Axelrod

272.

"You never know what you can do until you try."

- William Cobbett

273.

"Twenty years from now you'll be more disappointed by the things you did not do than the ones you did."

- Mark Twain

274.

"Believe in yourself, take on your challenges, dig deep within yourself to conquer fears. Never let anyone bring you down. You got to keep going."

- Chantal Sutherland

275.

"If you can't do anything about it, then let it go. Don't be a prisoner to things you can't change."

- Tony Gaskins

276.

"Don't judge each day by the harvest you reap, but by the seeds that you plant."

- Robert Louis Stevenson

277.

"The measure of who we are is what we do with what we have."

- Vince Lombardi

278.

"A hero is someone who has given his or her life to something bigger than oneself."

- Joseph Campbell

279.

"Your present circumstances don't determine where you can go; they merely determine where you start."

- Nido Qubein

280.

"There is nothing impossible to him who will try."

- Alexander the Great

281.

"You can't go back and change the beginning, but you can start where you are and change the ending."

- C.S. Lewis

282.

"I can and I will. Watch me."

- Carrie Green

283.

"Try not to become a man of success, but rather, become a man of value."

- Albert Einstein

284.

"A winner is a dreamer who never gives up."

- Nelson Mandela

285.

"The only thing standing in the way between you and your goal is the BS story you keep telling yourself as to why you can't achieve it."

- Jordan Belfort

286.

"With self-discipline, most anything is possible."

- Theodore Roosevelt

287.

"What we think, we become."

- Buddha

288.

"Happiness is not something you postpone for the future; it is something you design for the present."

- Jim Rohn

289.

"If you accept the expectations of others, especially negative ones, then you never will change the outcome."

- Michael Jordan

290.

"The best way out is always through."

- Robert Frost

291.

"Only do what your heart tells you."

- Princess Diana

292.

"If it's a good idea, go ahead and do it. It's much easier to apologize than it is to get permission."

- Grace Hopper

293.

"I attribute my success to this: I never gave or took an excuse."

- Florence Nightingale

294.

"The question isn't who is going to let me; it's who is going to stop me."

- Ayn Rand

295.

"A surplus of effort could overcome a deficit of confidence."

- Sonia Sotomayer

296.

"If you always put limit on everything you do, physical or anything else, it will spread into your work and into your life. There are no limits. There are only plateaus, and you must not stay there, you must go beyond them."

- Bruce Lee

297.

"Follow you bliss, and the universe will open doors where there were only walls."

- Joseph Campbell

298.

"I believe every human has a finite number of heartbeats. I don't intend to waste any of mine."

- Neil Armstrong

299.

"We can change our lives. We can do, have, and be exactly what we wish."

- Tony Robbins

300.

"What we need is more people who specialize in the impossible."

- Theodore Roethke

301.

"And, when you want something, all the universe conspires in helping you to achieve it."

- Paulo Coelho

302.

"I can be changed by what happens to me, but I refuse to be reduced by it."

- Maya Angelou

303.

"It's the possibility of having a dream come true that makes life interesting."

- Paulo Coelho

304.

"Don't compromise yourself. You're all you've got."

- Janis Joplin

305.

"When something I can't control happens, I ask myself: where is the hidden gift? Where is the positive in this?"

- Sara Blakely

306.

"One today is worth two tomorrows."

- Benjamin Franklin

307.

"Live your beliefs, and you can turn the world around."

- Henry David Thoreau

308.

"Each day provides its own gifts."

- Marcus Aurelius

309.

"Shoot for the moon, and if you miss you will still be among the stars."

- Les Brown

310.

"Your big opportunity may be right where you are now."

- Napoleon Hill

311.

"Doubt is a killer. You just have to know who you are and what you stand for."

- Jennifer Lopez

312.

"Be a first rate version of yourself, not a second rate version of someone else."

- Judy Garland

313.

"Learn from the mistakes of others. You can't live long enough to make them all yourself."

- Eleanor Roosevelt

314.

"Done is better than perfect."

- Sheryl Sandberg

315.

"What hurts you, blesses you."

- Rumi

316.

"Love and desire are the spirit's wings to great deeds."

- Johann Wolfgang Von Goethe

317.

"If we did all the things we are capable of, we would literally astound ourselves."

- Thomas A. Edison

318.

"Men must live and create. Live to the point of tears."

- Albert Camus

319.

"We have it in our power to begin the world over again."

- Thomas Paine

320.

"Most of us have far more courage than we ever dreamed we possessed."

- Dale Carnegie

321.

"A man is not finished when he is defeated. He is finished when he quits."

- Richard Nixon

322.

"The world is changed by your example, not by your opinion."

- Paulo Coelho

323.

"Be silly, be honest, be kind."

- Ralph Waldo Emerson

324.

"It's not what happens to you but how you react to it that matters."

- Epictetus

325.

"The best way to predict your future is to create it."

- Abraham Lincoln

326.

"From a small seed a mighty trunk may grow."

- Aeschylus

327.

"What we achieve inwardly will change outer reality."

- Plutarch

328.

"All you need is the plan, the roadmap, and the courage to press on to your destination."

- Earl Nightingale

329.

"What great thing would you attempt if you knew you could not fail?"

- Robert H. Schuller

330.

"Nurture your mind with great thoughts. To believe in the heroic makes heroes."

- Benjamin Disraeli

331.

"Successful people are not gifted; they just work hard, then succeed on purpose."

- G.K. Nielson

332.

"Don't watch the clock. Do what it does. Keep going."

- Sam Levenson

333.

"You can't have a million-dollar dream on a minimum wage work ethic."

- Unknown

334.

"Falling down is how we grow. Staying down is how we die."

- Brian Vaszily

335.

"There may be people that have more talent than you, but there's no excuse for anyone to work harder than you."

- Derek Jeter

336.

"The best preparation for tomorrow is doing your best today."

- H. Jackson Brown Jr.

337.

"Change your thoughts and you change your world."

- Norman Vincent Peale

338.

"Don't limit yourself. Many people limit themselves to what they think they can do. You can go as far as your mind lets you. What you believe, remember, you can achieve."

- Mary Kay Ash

339.

"The limits of the possible can only be defined by going beyond them into the impossible."

- Arthur C. Clarke

340.

"When you have a dream, you've got to grab it and never let go."

- Carol Burnett

341.

"The adventure of life is to learn. The purpose of life is to grow. The nature of life is to change. The challenge of life is to overcome. The essence of life is to care. The opportunity of life is to serve. The secret of life is to dare. The spice of life is to befriend. The beauty of life is to give."

- William Arthur Ward

342.

"The two most important days in your life are the day you're born, and the day you find out why."

- Mark Twain

343.

"You don't get paid for the hour. You get paid for the value you bring to the hour."

- Jim Rohn

344.

"Work hard and don't give up hope. Be open to criticism and keep learning. Surround yourself with happy, warm, and genuine people."

- Tena Desae

345.

"You can control two things: your work ethic and your attitude about anything."

- Ali Krieger

346.

"If you believe in yourself and have dedication and pride – and never quit, you'll be a winner. The price of victory is high, but so are the rewards."

- Bear Bryant

347.

"I have always believed, and I still believe, that whatever good or bad fortune may come our way, we can always give it meaning and transform it into something of value."

- Hermann Hesse

348.

"Reach for it. Push yourself as far as you can."

- Christa McAuliffe

349.

"Man never made any material as resilient as the human spirit."

- Bernard Williams

350.

"A champion is someone who gets up when he can't."

- Jack Dempsey

351.

"If you can't make a mistake, you can't make anything."

- Marva Collin

352.

"You may be disappointed if you fail, but you'll be doomed if you don't try."

- Beverly Sills

353.

"If we wait until we're ready, we'll be waiting for the rest of our lives."

- Lemony Snicket

354.

"Study while others are sleeping; work while others are loafing; prepare while others are playing; and dream while others are wishing."

- William Arthur Ward

355.

"The best revenge is massive success."

- Frank Sinatra

356.

"When the going gets tough, the tough get going."

- Joe Kennedy

357.

"Always make a total effort, even when the odds are against you."

- Arnold Palmer

358.

"Don't wait for your feelings to change to take the action. Take the action and your feelings will change."

- Barbara Baron

359.

"Success comes from having dreams that are bigger than your fears."

- Bobby Unser

360.

"Never do tomorrow what you can do today. Procrastination is the thief of time."

- Charles Dickens

361.

"If there is no wind, row."

- Latin Proverb

362.

"A goal is a dream with a deadline."

- Napoleon Hill

363.

"Everyone thinks of changing the world, but no one thinks of changing himself."

- Leo Tolstoy

364.

"The secret of change is to focus all your energy, not on fighting the old, but on building the new."

- Socrates

365.

"Your positive action combined with positive thinking results in success."

- Shiv Khera

Conclusion

Thanks again for choosing this book of 365 inspirational quotes!

I hope that you have enjoyed the quotes contained within, and that they have been able to provide you with a boost of motivation when you needed it most.

If you enjoyed this book, please don't hesitate to share it with your family and friends, and spread the inspiration around!

www.ingramcontent.com/pod-product-compliance
Lightning Source LLC
LaVergne TN
LVHW011720060526
838200LV00051B/2977